Bing™ Bears

Bing™ Bears

& Toys

Schiffer Publishing Ltd

4880 Lower Valley Road, Atglen, PA 19310 USA

Ken Yenke

Designed by Bonnie M. Hensley
Type set in Americana XBd BT/Zapf Humanist 601 BT

ISBN: 0-7643-1115-8
Printed in China
1 2 3 4

Published by Schiffer Publishing Ltd.
4880 Lower Valley Road
Atglen, PA 19310
Phone: (610) 593-1777; Fax: (610) 593-2002
E-mail: Schifferbk@aol.com
Please visit our web site catalog at **www.schifferbooks.com**

In Europe, Schiffer books are distributed by Bushwood Books
6 Marksbury Avenue Kew Gardens
Surrey TW9 4JF England
Phone: 44 (0)208-392-8585; Fax: 44 (0)208-392-9876
E-mail: Bushwd@aol.com
Free postage in the U.K., Europe; air mail at cost.

This book may be purchased from the publisher.
Include $3.95 for shipping. Please try your bookstore first.
We are always looking for authors to write books on new and related subjects.
If you have an idea for a book please contact us at the address above.
You may write for a free printed catalog.

Dedication

This book is dedicated to Eric and Margot Kluge, especially for their work in reviving the Bing Company. Eric's desire to share the Bing history and tradition is what led him to me, and this book is the result.

ontents

cknowledgments

This book is authorized by Gebr. Bing Inc. Eric and Margot Kluge, owners of Gebr. Bing Inc., have provided me with wonderful material and archival information.

Hilde Weidlich-Dittkowski, granddaughter of Kunz Weidlich, graciously shared information and drawings from her father, (Hermann) and grandfather (Kunz).

Reprints from Bing catalogs are credited to Ivan Steigers's Museum in Munich (Spielzeugmuseum in Alten Rathausturm Munchen).

All Bing items shown are from the author's collection, unless noted. Friends who graciously sent photos from their personal collection are: Chuck & Cathy Steffes; Lola's Antiques and Bears; Pat Beck; Rosmarie Binsteiner; David Douglas; Dick & Margie Motzer; Catherine (Sue) McKinney; Lenny Anderson; Barb Rivera; Michelle Borin; John Ormandy, and Chuck Meeks.

I would like to thank Peter Schiffer for his belief in, and understanding of, the importance of telling the "Bing" story.

Introduction

The Gebruder Bing company's story is a wonderful and remarkable tale. This toy company began production in 1865. Within a few short years, the firm is established as one of the premier toy manufacturers in the world. When Bing ceased operations in 1932, the company left a grand heritage to the entire world.

While this book is primarily about Bing teddy bears, I must acknowledge some of this manufacturer's other creations, which include: trains, automobiles, typewriters, sewing machines, phonographs, steam engines, and glass ornaments. The list goes on and on!

Yes indeed, Bing produced all of these toys and many more. Bing was truly at the pinnacle of the toy world in 1907, employing in excess of 6,000 workers. Their advertisements proudly proclaimed, "Bing, the Greatest Toy Factory in the World."

Fortunately for teddy bear lovers, Bing decided to enter into the "teddymania" market in 1906-07. The rest is history, and I am anxious to relay it to you.

For my part, it was providential that I happened upon "Austin" at a small Ohio auction. "Austin" is our 1907 Bing teddy bear, who led us dramatically into the wonderful world of Bing. For the purist collector, Austin is a 20" mint example, from 1907, with special order glass eyes, the first with the working growler, extra-long thick pile mohair and an original ear tag. In today's vernacular, this would be the ultimate teddy!

Erick Kluge, Bing's current owner and "reviver," saw pictures of Austin in a magazine article a few years ago. He contacted me to explore the possibilities of generating an inspiring look into the past, present, and future of the Bing Company.

Bing's original founders, their array of products, the artists who designed them, and the surviving treasures all serve to tell a dramatic story. The story of the wonderful world of Bing's teddy bears and toys, and of the rebirth of Bing.

Chapter I

History of the Bing Company

(1865-1932)

Ignaz Bing was born on January 29, 1840. At the young age of fourteen, Ignaz attended a business college. He would eventually graduate with top honors. Ignaz Bing gathered experience by serving an apprenticeship as a banker, which allowed him to travel throughout Germany.

In 1864, Ignaz started a wholesale clothing accessories business with his brother Adolf. Ignaz was also an experienced inventor familiar with cottage industry operations, and this experience led the partners into a new venture, metal accessories.

Adolf Bing was a very hardworking person, but lacked the vision of his brother. Adolf continually disapproved of any new ventures, and constantly cautioned Ignaz about his various business dealings. It was, however, Adolf's marriage into a very wealthy family that provided the extra capital for their business.

In 1865, the brothers Ignaz and Adolf Bing founded the Nuremberg Spielwarenfabrik "Gebruder Bing." This company was originally founded as a factory for kitchenware items and toys. Eventually items such as typewriters, stereopticons, and carburetors for cars and motorcycles could be found in Gebruder Bing's inventory. Their company flourished from its outset, and within less than two years the Bing brothers were employing over one hundred workers.

The German-French war of 1870 set Germany back economically; but, in spite of this adverse climate, Bing's business continued to expand. Ignaz took full advantage of the establishment of "common measurements," which were universally enacted throughout the German Empire. He made many contacts with key individuals and ultimately obtained the sole rights for supplying scales throughout Bavaria. Ignaz was also the recipient of a very distinguished honor. Prince Leopold, the Bavarian Ruler at the time, named Ignaz as the "Honorable Trade Counselor."

Ignaz was indeed the key individual at Gebruder Bing. It is noteworthy that he was, among other things, a very devoted explorer of his homeland. In the summer of 1905, he was credited with the discovery of one of the most beautiful stalagmite caves in Bavaria. Today it is possible to visit this glorious wonder, named Bing-Cave.

The Bing brothers were products of a very hardworking Jewish family. As an industrialist, Ignaz recognized the great value of each employee. His special treatment of them was rewarded, and his employees never went on strikes. During these years of the Industrial Revolution, Bing was instrumental in seeing that working conditions were constantly improved.

In only a few years, factory extensions were built to allow the firm to specialize in various production techniques. One extension was for enameled toys, such as boats and ships. By 1907, the teddy bear "rage" was reaching a peak worldwide. Bing was beginning its very own special production of plush animals. The Bing brothers used mohair and excelsior in creating their unique bears. People from all around began taking special notice when the Bings started incorporating their knowledge of mechanical mechanisms into their teddy bears.

Bing's mechanisms ranged from the very primitive "bobbing-head" bears, which used a simple weight, to the ultra-sophisticated walkers, climbers, and skaters. The Bing Company possessed numerous patents for their mechanical toys. The identification mark could be found on small medallions which were affixed to each product. "DRPa DIV DRGM" was the patent logo which was shown on each of these medallions.

> *Opposite page*
> Three rare 8" Bing teddies. None have pads on their arms, but all have felt pads on their feet. Blocks are each 3" tall.

From 1905-1909 Bing was a flourishing company. Over 6,000 employees and still growing, they continued to concentrate on perfecting their clockwork (wind up) mechanisms. This helped create great success in their export division. They established specialized outlets for their authorized dealers, which not only displayed all the marvelous and complex toys, but also repaired them on the spot! Specialized packaging, unique displays, and appealing products brought rave reviews from dealers.

Ignaz Bing died in 1918. His company had survived the First World War without any major damage, and his son Stephan would take over the management of Bing-Werke in 1919. G.B.N. (Gebruder Bing Nuremberg) is re-designated, without Gebruder (brother) and is named Werke (Company).

The early 1920s provided more of the successes which Bing had seemed to have from the very

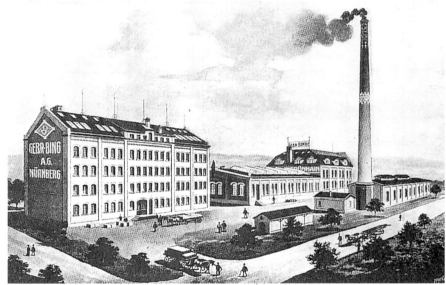

Bing Factories, 1912.

Picture of Ignaz Bing.

start. With the year 1927 came a very major change for the BW (Bing-Werke). Stephan Bing, and all other family members, separate themselves from their company. Although there are countless reasons offered for this separation, some as trite as plain disagreements about policy and management's style, the "root" problem was Germany's Adolf Hitler.

My research, and conversations with local historians, help us focus on the real events of that time. The entire Jewish community was blamed, by Hitler, for Germany losing World War I. Remember, Bing's company prospered after the war. However, Hitler's actions eventually forced the Bing-Werke out of business. The secret police not only took their property, but ultimately seized the owners. The entire Jewish culture in Germany was disrupted, to say the least. Contracts went anywhere else, but not to a Jewish firm like Bing. Strict boycotts were enforced. Eventually Bing and many other Jewish firms were closed down and dismantled.

In the ominous year of 1932, all of Bing's tools and machinery went up for auction. Countless firms lined up to place their bids on the treasures created by Bing.

Recognizable names used their auction acquisitions to keep Germany at the forefront of the toy industry. Bing's tools and toys went to firms such as Fleischmann, Bub, Schuco, Kraus, Trix, Fuchs and Bolz.

One final note: it was relayed to me that Hitler actually chose the city of Nuremberg as his official Parade Ground. The Gebruder Bing toy factory was part of the area taken over for that purpose.

On a much brighter note, let us preview some of the wonderful creations of Gebruder Bing. I have chosen a few of my favorites to lead us from Bing's history, to those who designed their teddies and toys. Treasures all!

The 1905 scene when Ignaz Bing discovered the cave that would carry his name.

Mechanische Spielwaren.

82/15/1 Gans mit Uhrwerk
mit beweglichen Flügeln, fein lackiert,
16 cm lang, 9 cm hoch,
per Stück **Mk.** —.38 | Pckg. 6

82/15/2 Hahn mit Uhrwerk
mit beweglichen Flügeln, fein lackiert,
14 cm lang, 10 cm hoch,
per Stück **Mk.** —.38 | Pckg. 6

82/15/3 Ente mit Uhrwerk
mit beweglichen Flügeln, fein lackiert,
14 cm lang, 10 cm hoch,
per Stück **Mk.** —.38 | Pckg. 6

82/17 Taube mit Uhrwerk
fein lackiert,
17 cm lang, 13 cm hoch,
per Stück **Mk.** —.38 | Pckg. 6

82/18 Katze mit Uhrwerk
mit beweglicher Maus, fein lackiert, mit
origineller Bewegung, 24 cm lang,
12 cm hoch, p. St. **Mk.** —.38 | Pckg. 6

82/16 Hahn mit Uhrwerk
mit festen Flügeln, fein lackiert,
16 cm lang, 13 cm hoch,
per Stück **Mk.** —.38 | Pckg. 6

82/19 Knabe im Fahren Kugel
drehend, mit Uhrwerk, fein lackiert,
20 cm hoch,
per Stück **Mk.** —.38 | Pckg. 6

82/24 Affe auf Esel
mit Uhrwerk, fein lackiert,
mit origineller Bewegung,
15 cm hoch, per Stück **Mk.** —.38 | Pckg. 6

82/20 Bär mit Uhrwerk
Kugel schlagend, fein lackiert,
13 cm hoch,
per Stück **Mk.** —.38 | Pckg. 6

Neben dem Preis ist die Packungsweise nach Stückzahl bezeichnet, unter welcher kein Artikel abgegeben wird.

---

20 h

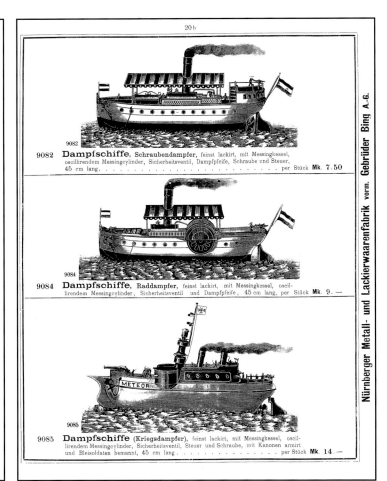

Nürnberger Metall- und Lackierwaarenfabrik vorm. Gebrüder Bing A.-G.

9082 Dampfschiffe, Schraubendampfer, feinst lackirt, mit Messingkessel, oscillirendem Messingcylinder, Sicherheitsventil, Dampfpfeife, Schraube und Steuer, 45 cm lang . . . . per Stück **Mk. 7.50**

9084 Dampfschiffe, Raddampfer, feinst lackirt, mit Messingkessel, oscillirendem Messingcylinder, Sicherheitsventil und Dampfpfeife, 45 cm lang, per Stück **Mk. 9.—**

9085 Dampfschiffe (Kriegsdampfer), feinst lackirt, mit Messingkessel, oscillirendem Messingcylinder, Sicherheitsventil, Steuer und Schraube, mit Kanonen armirt und Bleisoldaten bemannt, 45 cm lang . . . . per Stück **Mk. 14.—**

Elektrische Strassenbahnen für Schwachstrom
mit Permanent-Magnet-Motoren

mit Vorrichtung für **Vor-** und **Rückwärtsfahrt** mittels Stromwenders. Elemente und Akkumulatoren s. Seite 293 u. 294, Umschalter s. Seite 325.

Spurweite 00 = 28 mm
Zulässige Spannung 2—3 Volt, Stromverbrauch zirka 0,25 Ampère.

179/45/00

179/52/00 mit Anhängewagen
179/50/00 ohne Anhängewagen

Billige, elektrische Bahnen (Straßenbahnen) mit Schmalspurschienen, für **Vor-** und **Rückwärtsfahrt** eingerichtet, mit Schienenkreis inkl. Anschlußschiene.

179/45/00 Triebwagen 16 cm lang . . . . per Stück (ohne Element und ohne Umschalter) Mk. 4.90
„ /50/00 **ohne Anhängewagen**, Triebwagen 16 cm lang „ „ „ „ „ „ „ 4.80
„ /52/00 Triebwagen **mit Anhängewagen**, Zuglänge 34 cm „ „ „ „ „ „ „ 6.30

Spurweite 0 = 35 mm
Zulässige Spannung 3—4,5 Volt, Stromverbrauch ca. 1 Ampère.

180/35/00

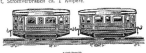
180/37/0

180/35/00 ohne Anhängewagen, mit Schienenkreis (4 gebogene Schienen inkl. Anschlußschiene),
15 cm lang . . . . per Stück (ohne Element und ohne Umschalter) Mk. 9.30
180/37/0 mit 1 Anhängewagen mit Schienenoval (4 gebogene, 4 gerade Schienen inkl. Anschlußschiene),
Zuglänge 33 cm . . . . per Stück (ohne Element und ohne Umschalter) Mk. 13.50

=== **Mit elektrischer Beleuchtung** ===

180/39/0 Motorwagen mit **elektrisch beleuchteter Stirnlampe** (Metallfadenlampe), Anhängewagen mit **elektrischer Beleuchtung im Innern**, mit Schienenoval (6 gebogene, 4 gerade Schienen inkl. Anschlußschiene),
35 cm lang . . . . per Stück (ohne Element und ohne Umschalter) Mk. 19.50
Zulässige Spannung 3,5—5 Volt, Stromverbrauch ca. 1,2 Ampère.

10217	**Metallfaden-Glühlampen** mit Zwerggewinde, 3,5 Volt, 0,25 Ampère, zur Stirnlampen-Beleuchtung für obige Bahn passend . . . . per Stück inkl. Steuer Mk. 1.—

Top left: An 1898 Bing catalogue page showing a mechanical bear.

Top right: An 1898 catalogue page showing early steam boats.

Bottom left: A 1912 catalogue page showing the HO scale invented by Bing.

Steam Engines with Models.

13934
13934 Factory
complete with Steam Engine and Models,
consisting of:
Steam Engine with oscillating brass cylinder, oxydized brass boiler, safety valve and steam whistle. The
Shafting works: 1 lathe, 1 grindstone, 1 drilling machine and 1 hammerwork, pulley wheels adjustable
with wedge lock, mounted on wooden board.
16¼ in. long, 8¾ in. wide, 14¼ in. high . . . . each **33/8**

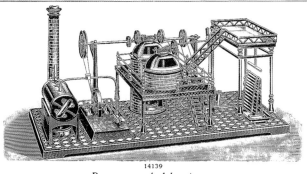

14139
Brewery, worked by steam,
mounted on firm wooden base
Superior Steam Engine with oscillating brass cylinders, oxydized brass boiler, safety valve, steam whistle,
all fittings finely nickelled, chimney stamped and finely japanned (imitation brickwork).
Brewery nicely japanned, exceedingly well finished; all machineries, which are connected with a brewery,
are exactly imitated, such as mash-charger, mash-cooler, brewing-vat, etc. etc. with copper fittings
19⅞ in. long, 9 in. wide, 11 in. high . . . . each **42/—**

A 1906 catalogue page of early steam engines.

A 1906 catalogue page of "modern cars."

A 1906 catalogue page of Christmas ornaments.

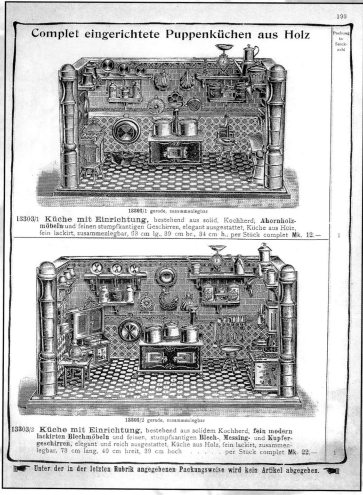

A 1906 catalogue page of a doll-sized kitchen.

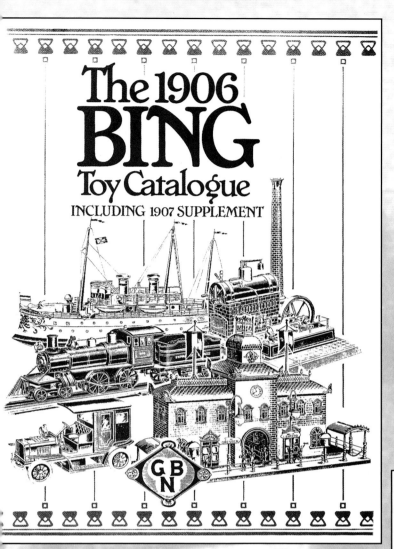

The 1906 catalogue cover.

A 1908 Teddy Bear catalogue page.

278a

Neue Spezialität: **Weichgestopfte Plüsch-Tiere.**

Solideste Ausführung! ▭ Naturtreue Formen! ▭ Vorzüglichstes Ia. Plüschmaterial.

☞ Marke ▭⬤▭ unterm Arm." ☜

Plüsch-Bären.

Mit Stimme

Sitzhöhe	No. für weiss	goldgelb	dunkelbraun	Preis per Stück
15 cm	280/10/15	280/11/15	—	Mk. 1.40
17 »	» /17	» /17	—	» 1.60
22 »	» /22	» /22	—	» 2.50

Mit automatischer Brummstimme

Sitzhöhe	No. für weiss	goldgelb	dunkelbraun	Preis per Stück
25 cm	280/10/25	280/11/25	—	Mk. 3.75
28 »	» /28	» /28	280/12/28	» 5.—
35 »	» /35	» /35	» /35	» 8.—

Neuheit!   Mit feinem Uhrwerk   **Originell!**

Kopf hin und her bewegend

(mehrere D. R.-G.-M. und D. R.-Patente angemeldet)

Sitzhöhe	No. für weiss	goldgelb	dunkelbraun	Preis per Stück
22 cm	280/20/22	280/21/22	—	Mk. 3.90
25 »	» /25	» /25	—	» 5.20
28 »	» /28	» /28	280/22/28	» 6.60
35 »	» /35	» /35	» /35	» 9.80

Mit elektrischem Antrieb

Kopf hin und her bewegend

für Schwachstrom zum Anschluss an Akkumulatoren (für **Schaufenster-Reklame**)

Sitzhöhe	No. für weiss	goldgelb	dunkelbraun	Preis per Stück
28 cm	—	—	280/32/28 ⎰ ohne Akku-	Mk. 12.—
35 »	—	—	» /35 ⎱ mulatoren	» 16.—

Für grosse Schaustücke (Auslagestücke) als Bärenzwinger etc. auf gefl. Verlangen Spezialofferte.

1908 D

19

Six wonderful early Bing teddies. Three in the front are 8" tall and date from 1907, 1910 and 1919. Value from $2,000 to $2,500 each. The two teddies behind them are 16" and 13" Bings from 1919 and 1907. The 16" white teddy is valued at $5,000. The 13" gold, with original ear tag, is $6,000. Standing in the back is our prize Bing named Austin. Measuring 20" tall, this mint original Bing from 1907, with ear arrow, is valued at $15,000+.

The six teddies are being circled by a Bing train from 1900. This clockwork locomotive, cars and accessories are worth $600+.

Teddy is on his feet, and still holds onto his honey. Notice the upper arms are nearly 1" longer than his legs. Mint condition value is $6,000.

A rare 13" Bing from 1907 sits atop a turn of the twentieth century honey can. Notice the brown-painted glass eyes on teddy, special order items in 1907.

First made in the 1890s by Bing, here we see their 1919 version of a hand operated miniature sewing machine. Measuring 9" long and 7" high, the sewing machine came with its own little vice to hold it onto a table. In perfect working condition, the value is $600+.

A side view of the miniature sewing machine gives us another look at the gold stenciling. BW is displayed in several areas on the base. I don't know its exact weight, but it is very heavy.

Guess what else Bing made...a milk-glass bird feeder. This one was found hanging on a turn of the twentieth century cage. Value is $100+ if you can ever find one. The bird feeder is 3" high.

When the bird feeder is hung on a cage, this side is accessible to the bird. Seed is poured inside this opening in the back.

A turn of the twentieth century Bing film projector. The projector is 9" long and 12" high. The value is $500.

Notice the brass fittings on the Bing projector. The bulb on top is an original light from 1914. It is marked Bing, Germany.

The 8", 1910 Bing teddy is looking for a little water. This Bing water tower is dated 1920. Value of the tower is $150.

Our little teddy stands at the water tower, cautious of the possible passing cars. This railroad crossing sign is from 1920. Its value is $50.

This magnificent typewriter works perfectly. Made in 1919, the metal cover forms the top of a convenient carrying case. Value is $300+. The typewriter measures 12" deep, 11" wide and 5" high.

The little clockwork locomotive is attended to by an 11" tall Bing character doll, both from 1920. The train is valued at $200. Doll is $250.

Chapter II

Designers Extraordinary

... the Weidlichs

Kunz and Herman Weidlich, father and son, were the renowned artists commissioned by Bing. They were responsible for the creation of countless toys and inventions.

Kunz Weidlich was born on May 5, 1878 and died on July 18, 1940. He was a painter in Nuremberg, renowned for his phenomenal portraits. Kunz was also famous as an inventor. In the city of Nuremberg, his ingenious inventions earned him the nickname of "Edison the Second."

His inventions were of the very practical nature. Kunz believed inventions "should serve as a tool to ease man's toil." Naturally, he specialized in areas such as household utensils and toys.

He owned fifty-five German and foreign patents. Fifty-one of them were actually produced and stocked in the major stores. Millions of these various articles were sold, including some very popular names, such as his "Kitchen Wonders." Among these we can include glass backing forms, cooking cabinets, ice cream making machines, coffee machines, fruit presses, and on and on.

One of the reasons that Kunz turned to inventing was the difficulty he had making a living as a painter. Being a painter was not a very typical profession during this particular time. Fortunately for Kunz, his sterling reputation gained him employment as a teacher to the royalty.

Kunz had the ability to do practically anything he wanted to do. If a mechanical instrument was difficult to operate, he could make it easy. His philosophy and talent led him to create his "For Every Man" utensils and toys.

Kunz Weidlich was indeed the very first professional designer for the toy industry. He was the father of the first artist-designed Bing teddy bears, appearing in 1907. Heinrich Mueller, founder of Schuco, was a student of Kunz Weidlich while he worked for Bing, prior to 1912.

Most of the wonderful drawings which appeared in the early Bing catalogues were done by Kunz Weidlich. His son, Herman, would join him at Bing, thus creating a dynamic duo. They were nicknamed the "Leonardo da Vincis."

Kunz excelled in creating animals. He employed a "designed from life" philosophy, as was stated on the cover of the 1914 toy catalogue advertisement.

Herman Weidlich, son of Kunz, seemed to inherit all of his father's talents. Born in 1899, in Munich, Herman was a mere eight years old when he received honorable mention for his drawings. This prize, from the mayor of Paris, would be the first of countless honors Herman would earn throughout his illustrious career.

Herman was schooled in both Nuremberg and Munich. Unfortunately, in a 1943 bombing raid, nearly 300 of Herman's paintings

A 1920s self-portrait of Kunz Weidlich.

were destroyed at his residence. He and his wife relocated to Bamberg, where his wife had been born.

While in Bamberg, the artist community recognized and accepted Herman's talents. By 1949, he had become Chairman for the professional federation of "Cultivated Artists." His achievements were similar to those of his father, and often you could not distinguish their work ... one from the other!

One of Herman's most notable achievements is his Coca Cola polar bear. He was the creator of the moveable, mechanical billboard. The drawing of the Coca Cola polar bears was

A 1914 catalogue ad page designed by Kunz Weidlich.

also done by Herman for those billboards. Notice that in the lower right corner of the picture presented, Herman's drawing contains the word "bottes" in-

stead of bottles! This is an original draft of that historic picture.

Herman died in 1956, at the age of 57. The legacy he and his father left with us is ever present within the Bing treasures.

Opposite page:
A 1924 painting by Kunz Weidlich.

Original Polar Bears designed by Herman Weidlich for a mechanical billboard.

Character "Sonny Boy" by Herman Weidlich.

Four captions of "Fighting Pollution," created by Herman Weidlich.

Sketch by Herman Weidlich.

Home of Hermann Weidlich & Hilde (daughter) in Bamberg.

Ken and Brenda shown with a 1914 Bing teddy bear.

Hilde Dittkowski-Weidlich, granddaughter of Kunz Weidlich, the original designer for Gebruder Bing. She is the daughter of Hermann Weidlich, designer for Gebruder Bing, who joined his father to create a design team at Bing. She is shown holding the 1909 replica Bing, introduced in 1995. The photo of the polar bears was created by her father in the 1940s for Coca Cola.

Old photo of the Weidlich home, and the city of Bamberg around W.W.II.

The original drawing by Hermann Weidlich for Coca Cola in Germany. This set of polar bears was designed for a mechanical billboard, which was also patented by the Weidlich's. Notice the word bottles is spelled "bottes" in this original.

An original drawing by the Weidlich's, used for the early Gebruder Bing catalogues. This small polar bear could be pulled along on small wheels.

Adult polar bear drawn for a 1912 Bing catalogue. This was the precursor of the Weidlich 1940s Coca Cola polar bears.

Another example of the early, turn of the twentieth century, design work by the Weidlich's. This realistic penguin was a clockwork walker. Drawn for a 1912 catalogue.

Called "Hare Babies," these humanized bunnies, with squeakier voice, were a plush design of the Weidlich's. Drawn for a 1908-1912 catalogue.

Boat with clockwork which pushes the boy, who has wheels on his feet. An original design by the Weidlich's. Drawn for a 1912 catalogue.

A walking duck, by means of clockwork mechanism, is shown in an original design by the Weidlich's. Drawn for a 1908-1912 catalogue.

Chapter III

Bing's Teddy Bears and Toys

This is the original tag used to mark the right ear of Gebruder Bing teddy bears. This metal tag was originally clamped into the ear seam, and bent over the outer portion of the ear. On some early "arrows," the word Bavaria is not printed, only the GBN. Used in 1907, it is extremely rare to find this in a teddy's ear today. Steiff's court order at that time forced Bing to remove this tag from their teddy's ear.

Gebruder Bing was officially founded in Nuremberg, Germany, in 1863. During their seventy years of production, Bing became recognized as the most prolific creators and manufacturers of toys in the world. It was the only toy factory which continued production during W.W.I.

As a genuinely dedicated antique (olde) teddy bear collector, I was to discover very early on that Gebr. Bing's excellence in toy making extended prolifically to teddy bears. Bing's teddies were not simple "copies," like those made by many other early entrants in the teddy-bear-mania. From the outset, their teddies uniquely displayed characteristics which to this day distinguish them from all others!

Bing's foresight to be the first teddy bear makers to hire outside, professional artists as their designers was key to their success. Exquisite life-like animals and bears resulted, with "Designed from life" as the original theme. Even now, nearly seventy years since they were last produced, collectors around the world are searching for the original Bing products. Premium prices are being paid for original Bing teddy bears as well as their other animals and toys. What better testament could there be to their artistic design and quality than to have today's collector's regard Bing toys as among the rarest and most desirable?

Nearly all the items you view within this book were found over the years, while I was searching for the Bing teddy bears. The wonderful clockwork trains, Bing sewing machine, typewriter, glass bird feeder, and more are all simple testimony to the grand Bing heritage.

I recently saw a Bing ship at auction, which brought $10,000. Don't expect to see that ship in this book! You will see wonderful examples of the more common toys of the day, which extend naturally to one's teddy bear collection.

There are magnificent examples of Bing toys in museums around the world. What you are about to view within these pages constitutes one of the best collections of Bing teddy bears you will have ever seen in one book. Many friends and fellow collectors have joined me in this effort, and have provided special photographs of their Bing teddy bears. Bing was indeed imitated, especially during the 1920s, and even more so after their dismantling in 1932. If imitation is the highest form of flattery, Bing is bursting with kudos.

The only way to truly share the Bing experience is to capture their uniqueness with photos of their varied designs. "Bear" in mind, all of the teddies and products shown are original and untouched. If there is any repair or change to a bear, I will tell you about it.

HOW DO WE KNOW IT IS A BING??

Let me count the ways!!

#1. Identifying Marks

Fortunately for us, Bing clearly marked nearly all of the toys that they produced. When we examine Bing teddy bears, or any of the other tin toys, we can look for sev-

The original "arrow" type tag shown in the right ear of a 1907 Gebruder Bing teddy bear.

eral basic marks. Probably the most crude identification is a basic ink stamp, which was used quite often on the tin toys. This stamp will say GBN (Gebruder Bing Nuremberg) if the product was made prior to 1918. Often times another stamp is found with this, and it will read GERMANY, or Bavaria.

The later stamp-pad type of mark will be the BW (Bing Werke), which indicates a manufacture date of 1919 or later. It should be obvious to anyone who has found toys with these stamps that the mark is anything but permanent.

When metal products are "permanently" identified, you will see the GBN or BW actually embossed into the metal, and the characters are raised. This Braille effect was most often used around 1900.

With glass items, like the milk-glass bird feeder, the letters BW were raised on the glass, as was the name Germany.

Once in a great while we are fortunate to have the company's name printed out for us. This could be in the form of raised painted metal on a train, or an artistic hand painting, as seen on railroad items. Usually the BING name is found on these various items, but many times the German patent and registered pattern (DRGM) is found with it. Beautiful stenciling and enameling are trademarks of Bing. The child's record player, or "Bingola," is a prime example of

the extraordinary artwork used on their products.

Teddy bears and assorted plush animals were clearly marked. There are five (5) basic marks that were used between 1906 and 1932. Each of the five metal

Sitting proudly, "Austin" displays the tag in his right ear. This 20" original Gebruder Bing teddy is one of the rare original specimens, preserved in his 1907 splendor.

tags clearly define when the product was marketed. Look for these metal tags, or partial tags, which will help you with identification.

The original tag used by Gebruder Bing to identify their teddy bear was in the form of an arrow. This tin arrow was clipped onto the right ear of the animal, much like farmers do to their livestock today (and did back in 1906). Written on this metal arrow was the word "Bavaria." Next to Bavaria is the logo GBN in a small triangle. This "arrow in the ear"

was indeed the first identification used on their Teddy Bears.

Steiff, the teddy bear maker in Germany, took Bing to court over the use of this arrow in the ear. Steiff claimed the ear was their territory and forced Bing to remove any remaining arrows from their teddy bears' ears.

Bing countered this by coming up with an embossed metal button, with the letters GBN inscribed upon it. These silver buttons were placed on the left side of the teddy's torso, just under where the left arm usually hangs. This silver "button" was very similar to the button used by

Steiff at that time, and once again Bing was forced to drop the name "button" from their catalogues and advertisements. It became known as the "mark under the arm." To this very day, this "button" ruling is held up against Bing. When Bing was the largest toy maker in the world in 1907, it employed twice the staff of Steiff. Perhaps this seemed a great threat to Steiff at the time, and consequently it was aggressively pursued.

The only other identification tag used by Gebruder Bing prior to World War I is the registration mark button. This tin button with

This is the early registration button used by Gebruder Bing. This tin button was placed under the left arm of teddy bears, sometimes in addition to the arrow clamped to the right ear.

a red background is found on teddies dating from 1908 onward. Sometimes the early items with the arrow in the ear also have this tin DRPa button on their torso. This button specifically denotes that Bing has filed official German patents on that particular teddy or plush toy. It is most often found on their clockwork acrobatic teddy bears, but as you will see, it is also on regular jointed teddies.

The most common forms of identification tags you will encounter are the red, blue, or white BW metal tags. These circular tags were clamped onto the right wrist of teddy bears. Usually the word GERMANY or BAVARIA was written just above the BW.

The early registration button is shown under the left arm of this 1908 teddy bear. In the right ear are the remains of half of a metal arrow, still held under the seam.

BW stands for Bing Werke (Works, or Company). GBN stands for Gerbruder (Brothers) Bing Nuremberg. After the death of Ignaz in 1919, the company was no longer operated by the brothers, so the name was officially changed to reflect this.

Dating of an item by the BW tags on the wrist is quite easy. The rarest of the tags after World War I would be the white one. I have only seen it on the miniature teddy shown herein, which dates from 1919.

The red tag, with either Germany or Bavaria appearing with the BW, marks the item from 1919 through 1927. The blue tag was the last form of identification used on plush teddy bears by Bing. This appeared up to their closing in 1932.

#2. Two Distinct Teddy Bear Styles

From the early teddy bear production years, Bing created two basic styles of teddy bears. Throughout the years, the distinguishing features and characteristics of these styles remain vivid.

The earliest catalogues showing their teddy bears clearly define the head and nose of their "sentry." These bears received the "sentry" name because they stand on tip toes, as if on watch, as a sentry. The long nose, and tip-toe style stance are defining characteristics as clear as any button or tag could be! From 1908 through 1925, this sentry style changed slightly to become what is thought of as the traditional style. The traditonal style bear stands flat footed. No sentry tip toe stance for this teddy bear. Also, the original ear placement was on the side of the head, similar to humans.

As the years passed, teddy had his ears move up onto the head, above the outside seems. This is the most noticeable change over those production years. The 1908 version closely resembles the "Margarete Strong" by Steiff. Clearly the traditional style was more closely aligned to the grand plush being offered by Steiff.

The extremely long arms, and artistically defined facial features clearly marked this second, or traditional, style of teddy. Each teddy communicates a uniqueness, not found on most other teddy bears. There are several major "early" teddy bear makers that have characteristics unique unto themselves. Bing teddies sit at the top of that list!

From their heads to their toes, we can find special traits to help us know these bears are Bings! The felt on the bottom of the foot forms a point at the heel. This is always the case when we are looking at the "sentry style" Bing. Sentry stands on his toes, and assumes a posture we often attribute to meer cats. The arms are not as long as the traditional style of Bing teddy bears. Usually the head has a more rounded design, and a long, exaggerated nose. The snout is usually shaved, which adds even more emphasis to its protrusion.

The nose stitching on all sentry style Bing bears is vertical, with a rounded stitch at the bottom. The size of the teddy doesn't change the direction of the stitch. No horizontally stitched noses appeared on sentry style Bings.

The eyes were usually blown glass, with large black pupils. The clear glass portion was painted brown. After W.W.I, the eyes remained the same, but the painted portion was an orange-brown.

Voices were usually tilt-forward growlers. These are commonly found in all sizes of teddy bears standing over 10" high. I have never encountered a squeeze type voice on any sentry style of Bing Teddy.

The common or traditional styled Bing *(you can't refer to any Bing as common)* conformed in several ways to the early Steiff teddy bears. The color of the nose stitching varied with the color mohair used on the bear. White teddy bears were given a light-cream colored stitching while gold colored bears received the traditional black stitched nose & claws.

Also, traditional style teddies with a size of 15" or less were given horizontally stitched noses, while those teddies with 16" height or better, received the vertical stitch.

Originally, shoe button eyes were the norm, but special order glass eyes were available. The eyes were blown glass, with large black pupils and brown painted glass. The glass eyes are much more predominant on a teddies face, which tend to communicate spectacular glances to passers-by.

The head is more squared, with the ears on the earliest bears sewn just below the upper head seams. As mentioned earlier, the ears kept moving toward the top of the head. Final production, around 1930-31, clearly have the ears sitting atop the head, inside the head seams. Glorious looks emanate from each teddy bear's face. When we imagine the artist's talent that created these treasures, we are in awe.

Explore the treasures that abound within these pages. Some were made over ninety years ago; the youngest teddy shown was going on sixty-five when this book was written!

These teddies and toys have provided countless years of enjoyment, and they keep on giving today!

A beautiful acrobatic 12" Bing is shown hanging from a tree branch. This popular clockwork somersaulter from 1909 is often found with a registration tin button under his left arm.

 A closer look reveals the early registration tin button under the left arm.

 Silver GBN button positioned under the left arm of a 1909 Bing teddy bear.

 Another look at the silver GBN button used under the arm.

This is the silver GBN engraved button which Bing finally put under the left arm of its teddy bears. It was originally called a button, but once again, Steiff's court order forced Bing to call it a mark, and place it under the arm, not in the ear. Used from 1908-10.

In 1919, after W.W.I and the death of Ignaz Bing, the Gebruder Bing of Nuremberg became known as Bing Werke. The red tin button, shown here, was displayed from that date forward. You will find this on the right arm of Bing teddy bears, usually in the wrist area. The name GERMANY, or BAVARIA, could appear with the BW.

The captivating look of this 1919 Bing teddy is prize-worthy. Shown on the right wrist, this 16" beauty displays a red BW metal tag.

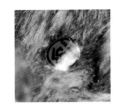

Shown on the right wrist is the blue tin BW tag which says GERMANY.

A closer look at the red BW tag on this 1919 teddy's arm.

Another version of the BW red tag is displayed by this 8" tumbling bear. "Made in Bavaria" is printed above the BW.

This blue BW tin button was the last form of identification used in Bing teddy bears. From 1927 through 1932, this blue tag was clamped to the wrist.

Identification can be done by ear design. Notice the small bear's ear, which is "sliced into" the bear's head. Only Bing sewed on the ear to this early primitive body style. Petz Co. sliced in the ear for quicker production. (The early peanut shaped body was created in Germany.)

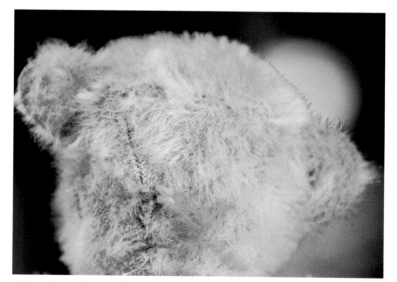

This photo displays the very small ears on the 1908 Bing shown. They are sewn on the side of the head, which indicates the early years.

Bing invented a "cut-in" ear design. The pattern is cut in such a way that an ear is incorporated into the design without any seams. It is actually part of the original face pattern. Only Bing used this, and it is found on very few teddy bears. 1908-1910 seems to be the time it was done. Not all 1908-1910 teddies have this style ear. Very rare.

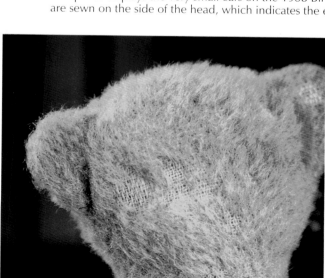

Another view of the rare ear pattern used by Bing. This 1908 brushed wool 8" teddy has ears that have no seams. Very unique design.

Identification can extend to many areas. This 6" white mohair Bing dates from 1911. He is pin jointed (wired), and has a metal body. It appears to be a predecessor to the Schuco, which appeared 15 years later. The little feet seem to be standing on their toes. This is one of the distinct Bing styles, in addition to the stately snout.

Laying face down, this 1912 Bing teddy gives us a chance to learn another means of identification. The heels of the feet have the felt sewn to a point. Every 1912 through 1925 tip-toe, or sentry style, Bing I have ever seen has this foot pattern design.

The traditional style Bing teddy bear displays the ankle design. The ankle shown is from 1919, its owner is 16" tall.

43

Faces tell the whole story. This is a wonderful 16" Bing from 1919. Notice the ears are slightly above the seams on the side of the head. Painted glass eyes, and vertically stitched nose are prominently shown.

Beautifully designed 9" Bing from 1919. The horizontal nose pattern is typical for a teddy of less than 15" height. Glass eyes are original, and a bit larger than would be the norm. This over-sized eye lends an alert sweetness to teddy.

This 1990s Bing is one of the 90th anniversary teddies. In keeping with the traditional style Bing, antique mohair, tilt growler, and properly stitched nose accent this replica. Shown are black frosted glass eyes, which are a special addition to this old style teddy bear.

Bing's 8" tumbler from 1919 is brown. This particular tumbler was probably made in 1910-1914 and tagged after the war. In addition to tiny sewn shoe buttons, he wears a perfect felt outfit. All of his cinnamon mohair is gone...aside from that he is perfect. The little horizontally stitched nose is fashioned of cord. Notice the little black thread above the eye and below the mouth stitch; without mohair you see where the cord was tied off.

The face of a 1912 Trippel-Trappel terrier exhibits brown painted glass eyes. Notice the vertically stitched nose which has two accented drop stitches on each side. This distinctive stitching was copied throughout the plush world at that time.

Dating from 1908, this small terrier has shoe button eyes and the classic Bing horizontally stitched nose. All original, we can distinguish the outline stitch around the nose.

45

Prior to 1900, we see very primitive designs. This mohair over mâché, bobbing head bear possesses a tin nose with painted nostrils.

The final chapter in the original Bing teddy bear line is shown here. This teddy was made in the late 1920s. The ears sit very high on the head, and the amount of cord used for the nose has greatly dwindled. Brown painted glass eyes offer a serious look.

Wow...what a nose.. all original, this beauty dates from 1910. Contrary to earlier opinions, this style did exist before the 1920s. As a matter of fact, this long nosed bruin was created in 1908. The style is called "Sentry." Huge glass eyes and a huge nose bridge mark this style, which was made into the early 1920s. He is a 24" teddy.

The large brown painted eyes look out over the proudly sewn, vertically stitched nose. Dating from 1919, this 16" teddy is undaunted by time's passage.

Standing 12" high, this golden Bing is very special. Remains of a metal arrow are in his right ear, giving us a clue to his early manufacture date. In front of his shoe button eyes sits a rust colored cord nose. One of the more meticulously stitched, notice the outline of the nose area.

Another distinctively long nose, this one resides on a 20" teddy from 1914. Beautiful apricot toned mohair, and more of an orange-brown painted glass eye. Artistically superb.

Savor the look of this original 1907 Bing teddy bear nose. The long slope of the nose is crowned with a nose that is a work of art by itself. Realistic, special order glass eyes gaze from the long cinnamon-honey mohair.

Sweet faced Bing from 1908. Brushed wool covered, the shoe button eyes are the smallest of the day. Ears are human-placed at the side of the head. His horizontally stitched nose is perfect, even after 90 years.

Dating from the 1920s era, the 20" bruin displays a magnificent face. Brown painted glass eyes, vertically stitched cord nose and ears located high on the teddy's head. The apricot highlights in the mohair are becoming.

This dark cinnamon mohair is especially eye catching. Ears are high atop this 14" teddy's head. Dating from the 1920s, his eyes have an orange cast to the paint. The nose is cord stitched with the horizontal pattern.

Dating from pre-1910, this small-faced teddy could not be any cuter. Tiny ears on the side of the head, shoe button eyes and a perfectly stitched horizontal cord nose are his attributes. Very special.

Bing created this face in 1907. A black curly mohair poodle stares at us with his orange-brown painted glass eyes. The black cord nose is highlighted with the pinkish cord mouth and nose outline. This dual color permits us to see exactly what is meant by the Bing outline stitch.

I have seen this exact bear pattern from both Bing and Steiff. This particular face is from Steiff, and the ear has an original button which helps us distinguish from Bing. The eyes and nose stitching are almost identical to Bing's for this style bear.

For comparison, this is the face of a 16" Steiff teddy from 1908. As seen, the face and nose have very similar characteristics.

One more comparison, this 18" Steiff from 1912 shows special order glass eyes. The realism, combined with a distinctive vertically stitched nose, offer us another teddy that closely resembles the early Bing look.

This artwork was created by Kunz Weidlich
for the 1908 Gerbruder Bing Catalogue.
One of the first teddy bear pages by Bing.

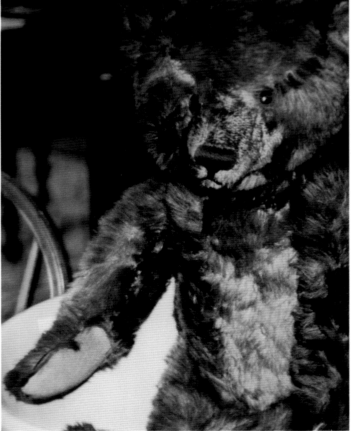

A close-up of one of the first Gebruder Bing teddy bears, covered
with 75 years of soot.

What a difference a shower makes. This was a diamond in the rough. Brenda spent one week gingerly cleaning him inch by inch. As I stated, the dust and soot provided a protective blanket from pests and discoloration. This "mint" 20" 1907 teddy has a working growler, and the original arrow marker in his ear. Value $15,000+.

Notice the arrow in his ear. Austin's hand painted glass eyes add another dimension to his wisdom. Here he reads "The ABC's in Pictures"

Inside this delightfully illustrated book, we find it was printed in the same year as Austin was born, 1907.

Austin is seen here featured on the cover of the Year 2000 Classic Bears calendar by American Greetings Corporation. © AGC. Inc.

Posing with his Year 2000 calendar portrait, Austin surely turned out to be a diamond in the rough.

This 20" beauty was produced in 1912. Highlights of the apricot mohair still are visible today. This is the sentry style, which features a rounded head and large nose. Value is $5,000+.

A look from another angle shows how prominent his head and nose are. The painted glass eyes add a special look.

Opposite page:
Standing to show his tip-toe design, we see a pair of sentry designed Bing teddies from 1912. Both have tilt forward growlers that work. This style of teddy was made before and after W.W.I. Value is $3,000+ each.

Three "sentry" or "tip-toe" style Bings. Two 12" and one 20".
Value of 12" is $3,000+ each. 20" is $5,000+.

Two buddies from the
1912-1914 era. These 12"
wonders are near mint.

The largest of the "Sentry" or "Tip-Toe" style Bing from 1912. At 24", he presents a dramatic look. Value is $7,500+.

Looking straight on, Mr. Bing offers his knowing glance.

One special look at three distinct sizes of the early Bing sentry style teddy bear. 12", 20", and 24". Notice the ears are on the side of the head, this indicates pre-W.W.I manufacture. Values: $3,000, $5,000, $7,500+.

Dating from nearly 1930, this 17" golden teddy marks the final style created by Bing. Value is $3,000.

This traditional Bing was sold just prior to Bing's closure in 1932. Ear placement is very high on his head, and the nose cord is not as thickly stitched.

One more look at this 1927-1932 Bing. He still has that great Bing head and body, with the prominent nose.

Opposite page:
The front view of the 20" Bing displays his magnificent appeal. Standing is a late 1920s, 17", perhaps the final production of Bing prior to 1932. Value is $3,000+.

Notice the nose on this 6" character. Heinrich Mueller worked for Bing until 1912, and was the pupil of Kunz Weidlich, the company's designer. This 1910 miniature Bing was the forerunner of the Schuco which came to fruition nearly 15 years later. Described as the Titanic bear, his value is $1,000+.

A front view of this 6" beauty captures more of his personality. This teddy is pin jointed (wire), and has a metal body covered with mohair. White mohair is another reason for his desirability.

This 20" Bing teddy dates from the 1920s. Value $4,000+.

The 20" from the late 1920s retains all the appeal of the earliest Bings. The ears are higher on the head. Value $4,000+.

One final glance displays the facial structure and stoic look of the late 1920s Bing.

The three bears shown are all pre-1910. Two are Bing, one is Petz, all have "peanut" styled bodies. The necks are not jointed, ergo the name peanut style. The 9" in the center is Petz, with sliced in ears. It is valued at $300+.

These two early Bings date from prior to 1910. The 4" miniature has hand painted glass eyes, a meticulously sewn nose, and the large ears are finely sewn to the top of this peanut styled body. Bing used pin joints for many early miniature bears and other animals. The small bear is the same one used on an early clockwork toy from Bing. Four of these little bears danced on wire poles when wound. The 16" teddy is the largest pin (wire rod) jointed Bing I have ever found. The bear has shoe button eyes, working push voice, heavy felt pads which are rarely found on this peanut style body. Rare in his form. The values are $500+ for the small bear, and $1,500+ for the rare 16".

A beautiful 16" cinnamon colored teddy from 1920. Value is $3,000+.

Shown from this side, we can distinguish the long arms, sharp looking nose design and thick torso.

Notice the foot design of the standard 16" teddy from 1920. Throughout that decade, this style was maintained.

Standing 14" tall, this cinnamon teddy was born in 1925. Value $2,500+.

Sitting, our 14" 1925 teddy displays his stout body, in nearly perfect condition.

Although this 9" teddy dates from 1919, his style goes back to 1908.

What a striking look...one of our favorites. The slightly over-sized glass eyes Bing used for this teddy, simply magnify his appeal. Value $2,000+.

A final glance at the 9" gives us an opportunity to notice the padless paws. This style was created in 1908, and briefly made after W.W.I.

Notice the great profile of the head and body on this 12" show stopper.

An original 1908 teddy, with the remains of an arrow in his right ear. Under his left arm is hidden the red patent registration metal button. He features all-in-one pattern ears, which are part of his head pattern, no paw pads, and tiny shoe buttons which make him desirable. Value $2,500+.

Opposite page:
An original 1908 12" Bing teddy, with shoe button eyes. In his ear remains part of the original tin arrow, and he has the great rust colored cord for his nose. Unusual, the value is $5,000+.

The large arm joints are prominent on this 1908 beauty. A boy teddy for sure.

A whole lot of teddy in a 12" body. Mint condition, value $5,000+.

At 12" tall, his joints are too loose to have him stand without assistance. Dating from prior to 1910, he has a sweetness to share. Value $3,000.

A side view displays the small ears and over-all proportions of this dainty teddy. He does have large feet...

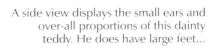

Our 12″ teddy with large feet needs "Bear Brand Hosiery."
Value of the hosiery box, with 6 pairs of socks is $300.

A final glance from this small featured Bing.
Value of teddy is $3,000.

For comparison, we are looking at a rare Steiff teddy from 1909-1912. Standing 18" tall, his value is $7,500+.

Notice the special glass eyes and long nose on this particular Steiff. Thank goodness for buttons and arrows to help us distinguish makers. Often, they are too close to call. There is a button in his left ear.

Opposite page:
Bing's wonderful tumbling bear, with hooks to hold him in position. Standing 12", with Bing's own clockwork design mechanism which is arm-wound, he is valued at $4,000+.

This is a 1908-1912 gymnast. When the arm is wound, he will turn somersaults. This design drawing by Kunz Weidlich would result in Bing's introducing the ACRO bear in 1908.

In excellent condition, his strong body is ready to perform.

Our cinnamon gymnast is ready to assume his position.

First he will stand on the red platform box. Our performer is about to attach his paw to one of the chains.

Standing at the ready, he must attach his other paw to begin.

With both arms attached, and pre-wound, he is ready to perform.

Teddy's head starts forward.

Slow and steady, that's our teddy.

Almost in the heels over head position.

Teddy is ready to complete his somersault.

Our gymnast has made his revolution, and prepares to dismount.

Standing on all fours, this looks as though he awaits our applause...

Kunz Weidlich's design drawing for the skating cat which was produced between 1908 and 1912.

The front view of our skater reveals the great likeness of this 1950 Schuco to the 1908 Bing. The torso is "peanut" style, the neck is part of the body, hidden by the factory included scarf.

Originally a Bing design from 1908, here we see the skating teddy. Standing 8" tall, this key wound bear will push himself along in a cross-country motion by using the stick. Schuco produced this in the 1950s from Bing designs. Mint value as shown is $2,000+.

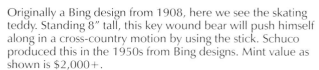

Another view with his original stick and chain, which is sometimes found attached to his metal nose.

Dating from the 1890s, this 8" Bing nodder is in wonderful condition. He will bob his head for several minutes with the slightest nudge. Value is $1,500+.

An original 1908 walking bear, with a metal GBN/Bavaria arrow in his right ear. This skating bear establishes the fact that the "peanut" style body was indeed created and used by Bing from around 1908 onward. Value $4,000+.

A Bing baby bear from around 1900. Inside is housed a Bing clockwork mechanism. When wound, the 8" bear bends slightly to his waist, and then slowly returns upright. Mohair over wood and mâché, with key wind. Value $1,500+.

A side view allows a different perspective. Notice the mousy ears, small metal nose, and curved arms. Circa 1900-1905.

The 1908 walking-skater by Bing pauses on a small bridge.

In the background sits the 1908 12" Bing gymnast who performed earlier. Sitting in the front, on his hands, is another performer. This 8" bear was designed in 1908, and produced from 1909 through 1920. All of the mohair from his paws, feet and head has disappeared. His clothes are perfect, and so is his mechanism. Value as shown is $3,000.

This little tumbler has had his arm wound, and he is ready to perform.

Notice the BW tag on his wrist, as he slowly does his first somersault.

Fully stretched, this little guy will tumble for several minutes.

He is showing off for you. Even without his mohair, this little tumbler displays loads of charisma.

A jumping frog clockwork toy as drawn by Kunz Weidlich.

This is a 1908-1912 design by Kunz Weidlich. This is a jumping monkey, which works from a Bing clockwork.

A jumping kangaroo was only natural.

Artistically illustrated jumping rabbits by Kunz Weidlich. 1908-1912.

Finely detailed tin auto with three rabbits, as detailed in 1908-1912 by Bings artist Kunz Weidlich.

Magnificent jumping hare from 1908. Standing 7" tall, with clockwork mechanism, bunny will hop across any table or floor. In wonderful condition, value is $2,500+. *From Barb Rivera's collection.*

A closer look at one of the very special Bing toys. White mohair, pin jointed arms, velvet on the inside of the ears, and an original felt outfit. *From Barb Rivera's collection.*

The stately Bing nose is proudly displayed.

A great study in the work of Kunz Weidlich. This 11" high and 14" long poodle was created around 1905. The long curled mohair was complimented with an all velvet body. The hand painted glass eyes, and barking voice make this dog a favorite of mine. Value $1,500+.

From the rear we see the body material, which originally was covered with velvet. Now the underbelly only has velvet.

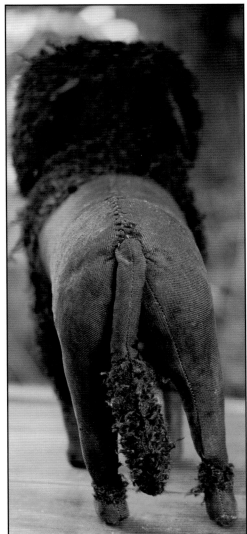

After 90+ years, this outstanding design attracts as many viewers as a fine painting would.

This bear on all fours, on wooden wheels, dates from 1920. I am showing you this Steiff, who has a button in his ear, to allow a comparison. Study the realistic design, it is very similar to Bings.

A view from this angle provides a better look at the body shape of this bear.

This real bear style was done exactly the same way by Bing. Steiff's bear shown is 8" tall, and 11" long. Value is $2,000+.

A magnificent wheeled bear design by Kunz Weidlich, circa 1908-1912.

A clockwork Bulldog drawn by Kunz Weidlich, circa 1908-1912.

Three puppies designed and drawn by Kunz Weidlich.

Mohair plush cats as interpreted in 1908 by Bing's designer.

Original drawing of a cat on wheels, with a rolling ball, 1908.

Clown cat with clockwork mechanism in the ball. Designed 1908.

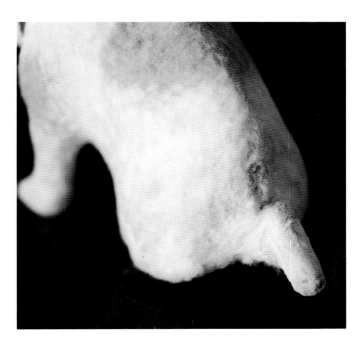

The tail on this bulldog is actually a plunger which produces a barking sound.

Splendid bulldog created by Bing in 1910. The body is felt covered and handsomely air brushed. Original collar and bell are part of this mint dog. The plunger tail works well. Value $500+.

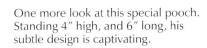

One more look at this special pooch. Standing 4" high, and 6" long, his subtle design is captivating.

Designed in 1908, this dog on wheels was made 25" long.

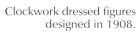

Clockwork dressed figures designed in 1908.

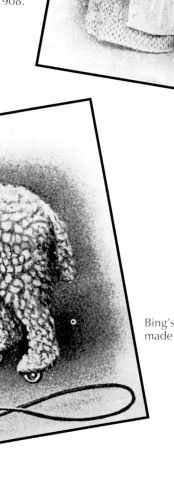

Bing's mohair sheep on wheels, made in 1912.

The artistry of Weidlich shows forth in yet another clockwork couple.

Woolly plush dog design from 1908.

Bing designed bell toys as early as the 1890s. Shown here is a 1908 toy which combines a plush dog with the bell toy.

A felt elephant with a bell toy. Bing's design, 1908-1912.

The bear pull toy created around 1900 by Bing. The mâché and wood bear is covered with mohair. The bell toy rings as you pull the bear along. In near mint condition, value is $2,000+.

The frontal photo displays the small wheel beneath the bear which permits the feet to stay just off the surface.

A final glance at our stately Bing bear bell toy.

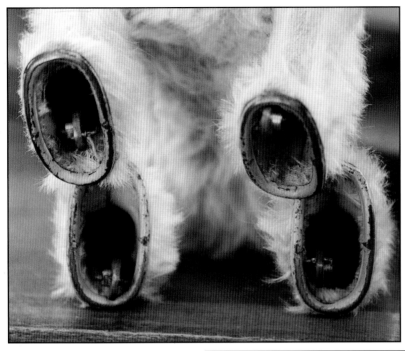

Notice the tiny wheel mechanism which causes the walking action of the Bing Trippel-Trappel animals.

Three wonderful Trippel-Trappel Bing terriers. The two on the left are 11″ long, the 7″ puppy on the right is quite different in appearance. All three dogs represent one of Bings greatest success stories. They created the mechanism, without any clockwork, that allows the dogs to walk with natural leg movement. Dating from 1908-1912, value is $750+ each.

The larger Trippel-Trappel terrier on the left displays hand painted glass eyes, and a vertically stitched nose. The puppy on the right has deep set shoe button eyes, and a very detailed horizontally stitched nose.

A close view of the box top for a Trippel-Trappel dog from 1908.

Vintage terrier sits atop his original box.

The artistry of Bing's designer is ever present, especially when viewing these three terriers.

This is the official tag created for the Trippel-Trappel animals. It usually hung around the collar of the animal.

This side of the tag names the product and notes registration.

Drawing from 1908 for a bear Trippel-Trappel.

Drawing from 1908 for a King Charles spaniel Trippel-Trappel.

Drawing for a 1908 catalogue. This depicts six different Trippel-Trappel animals being pulled by the clown in the center. Notice the drive wheel to the right which made the display work.

This is a felt covered bulldog in the Bing Trippel-Trappel line, 1912.

West Highland terrier design for the Trippel-Trappel line, 1908.

Pomeranian as designed in 1908 by
Kunz Weidlich for Bing.

Grey felt elephant designed for the
Trippel-Trappel line, 1908.

Black and white cat design
from 1912 by Kunz Weidlich
for Bing.

Bing produced countless tinplate toys.
Shown here is a coal shuffler from 1919.
Value with identification is $400.

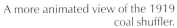
A more animated view of the 1919
coal shuffler.

The water mill toy dates from 1900.
Value with identification is $500.

The other side of this finely painted water mill from 1900.

Notice the fine detail of the operator. Oftentimes Bing would have three or more of these toys hooked to a long gear which caused them all to operate simultaneously.

The embossed BW marks the bottom of the 1919 coal shuffler.

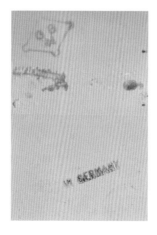

Under the water mill we find the earlier stamped logo from 1900.

Face to face, these two tinplate toys were produced from around 1900 through the 1920s.

Two remarkable Bing toys. Standing atop the turntable, is a rare 3 1/2" mohair cat. Bing made this cat around 1910. She has simple green glass eyes, and is pin or wire jointed at the arms and legs. The head is disc jointed. The air brushing is applied to the mohair before the cat is sewn. I have also had this small cat with black glass eyes. Value of this rare cat is $1,500. The Bingola child's record player is one of the most detailed and decorated I have ever seen. Marvel at the graphics! This key wind player is valued at $750+.

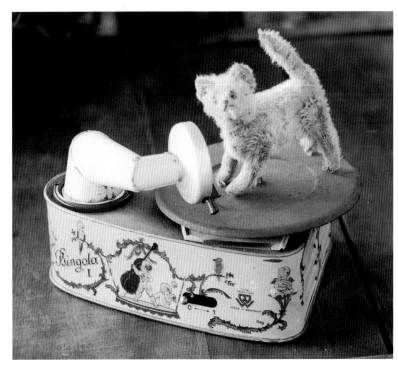

Our Bing companions display the diversity of this magnanimous toy producer.

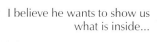

I believe he wants to show us
what is inside...

Standing 16″ tall, our 1920s cinnamon teddy
is showing off another of Bing's children's
record players. This one is called
Pigmyphone, or small phonograph. Bear's
value is $3,000+. Pigmyphone is $750+.

110

All the parts are neatly kept in the metal box.

As the lid is lifted, we see a self contained clockwork record player. This toy record player was first made by Bing around 1910, and was sold through the 1920s.

When wound, the clockwork mechanism allows a complete record to play through. Sounds are transmitted from the producer cylinder, through the small megaphone.

If you listen closely, you can here the words and music. "If you go down to the woods today, you'd better go in disguise."

It looks as though our 24" Bing teddy wants to hear his favorite tune. Here he chooses the Bingola as his instrument of choice. This toy record player from 1910 is graphically unequaled. Teddy's value $7,500+. Bingola's value $750+.

Very hard to find is the actual record sleeve from 1919.

Once more, it is a combination of toys, this teddy and his record player, that attest to Bing's legacy.

A close look at the record sleeve shows us a graphic look at the four different styles of children's record players that they made.

This closer look at the reverse side shows a list of a dozen vocal, and a dozen instrumental tunes available for any of the four styles of player.

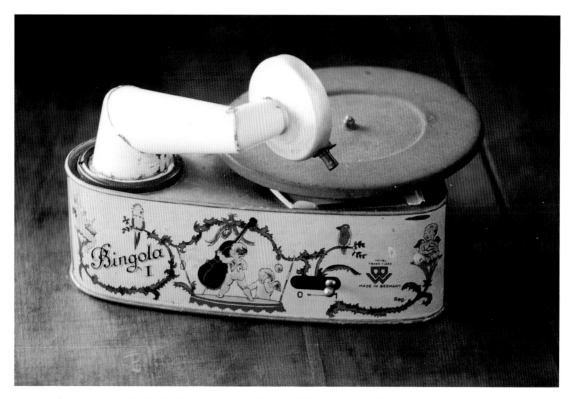

Probably the favorite graphics of all the Bing toys I have seen are shown here. The lever controls clockwork playing speed.

The reverse side is just as artistically done. The key wind is shown here.

This is a Bing stereopticon. Manufactured in 1898, it is valued at $200. Show in the viewer is a special scene. This is Teddy Roosevelt on a bear hunt in 1902. This particular stereo card is worth $100+.

A working Bing typewriter from 1920. Value is $250.

A perfect 20" 1907 teddy, Austin. Contrast the machining skills used to produce this working manual typewriter.

A picture is worth a thousand words.

One more pose. Thank you, Bing.

A 9" teddy from 1919, and his toy clock-work car from the same year. The teddy is valued at $2,000+. The auto is valued at $750+.

Notice the finely detailed driver, and the painted tire treads, still visible. This car was produced as early as 1905.

On the license plate you can see the BW (Bing Werke) logo.

As the car pulls away we can see another license plate with BW, from 1919.

Our 1912 sentry styled Bing teddy has put on his railroad outfit. Let's look at some of his train toys and accessories. Teddy is valued at $3,000+.

The impressed logo is seen on the bottom of this railroad car. The GBN (Gebruder Bing Nuremberg) and Bavaria indicate it was made before W.W.I.

A view from the other side of the tower shows the BW trade mark, and DRGM.

This railroad tower from 1920 carriers a scripted Bing, handsomely done.

A 10" station house had wonderful coloring. The BW logo is displayed. Value is $200.

This 8" train tower is valued at $100.

Measuring 8" across, this ticket office dates from 1920. Value is $150.

An original design by Kunz Weidlich in 1908 for Bing's catalogue.

Our 12″ and 20″ teddies from 1912 display a Bing clockwork train from 1920. Notice the BING logo on the locomotive. This train is from the John Ormandy collection. Value is $400.

Teddy and toy train.

Opposite page:
The three bears seem to be dressed in their railroad garb. That must mean we are going to play with trains.

A close look at the 1920 Bing wind-up train with coal car. From the John Ormandy collection.

A tiny white Bing teddy from 1912 plays with his tiny black Bing train.

Teddy has a better view from the Bing bridge. Value is $150 for the bridge.

124

Drawing found in a Bing toy engine house from 1905.

Here is the actual engine house today, with an engine in waiting. Value for the pair is $300.

The engine house dates from 1905 and has signs of wear. The Engine is crisp and mint, but dates from 1920.

Safely on the ground, the Bing brothers (Gebruder Bing) pose for your admiration.

Opposite page:
These two Bing brothers are enjoying the Bing bridge.

Our tiny peanut bodied Bing sits contentedly with his railway house. Teddy is pre-1910, the railway accessories are from 1920.

A glance at three cars and a tower from 1920. $400 value for all.

The newer identification is found on the 90th anniversary teddy.

Sitting atop the Bing box with the current logo, we find our 90th anniversary teddy.

The 90th anniversary replica teddy is shown with its photo, being held by Kunz Weidlich's granddaughter.

Sitting together we see the anniversary teddy with his counterpart from the late 1920s. Value of the 1920s teddy is $3,000+.

The glass medallion shows GBN, and Bing.

Under the arm we find a leather tag with GBN, and Bing listed. This teddy is hand numbered 777, and signed by Eric Kluge.

Spectacular opening photo from our friends. This 24″ Bing teddy is no Liberace, but certainly creates music. His audience consists of a 26″ Schoenau and Hoffmeister doll; a 1911 Schoenhut piano; a 15″ Kestner character baby from 1915; and a Heinrich Handwerke 26″ doll from 1900. *From the collection of Michelle Borin.* The Bing teddy is valued at $7,000+.

Chapter IV

Treasures from Friends

Teddy bears are wonderful contributors to the *human* experience. It is through the experience of collecting that we are able to meet wonderful teddy bears, and their owners! The mutual appreciation shared by fellow collectors serves to elevate and enhance every newly found treasure. I know I am not only entertained, but also learn much from each conversation I have with a friend who has "just added" to a collection.

Contained in this chapter are some special Bing teddy bears. By now it should be rather apparent that a Bing teddy from 1906 through 1932 is very desirable. Desirable, not only because they are such special works of art, but also because they were made in the early part of the twentieth century and are extremely scarce.

Over the past few years I have been fortunate to view an occasional Bing teddy bear within various collections. When asked, these owners responded in grand fashion. My request for a snapshot of their Bing resulted in a very special chapter in this book, *Treasures from Friends*.

Beautiful cinnamon mohair is shown on this 24" Bing from 1925. *From the collection of Chuck and Cathy Steffes*. His value is $7,500+.

Sitting beneath the pines. *From the Chuck and Cathy Steffes collection.*

Notice the large ears, sewn inside the head seem. This is one way of dating him to post-W.W.I. *From the Steffes collection.*

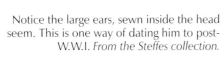

Great photo, showing the 24" Bing standing with great stature. He does have a blue BW tin button on his right arm. This dates him from the late 1920s to 1930. *From the Steffes collection.*

Sitting inside for this photo, teddy displays the deep rich tone to his mohair. *From the Steffes collection.*

Another view of one stately Bing. *From the Steffes collection.*

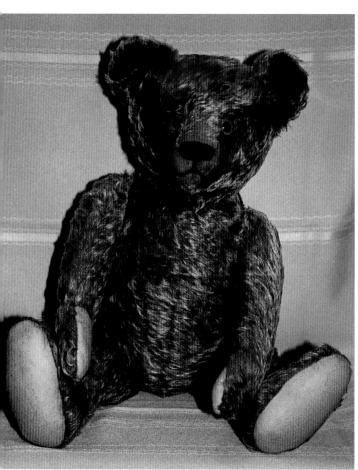

A final view shows the large feet, and a contrasting color found in the orange-painted glass eyes. *From the Steffes collection.*

Three of the most special Bing teddies. *From the Steffes collection.*

Three magnificent examples of Bing bears. *From the Steffes collection.* The dark brown bear is from 1920, and valued at $2,500+. The huge teddy in the center is 32" tall, from 1914-1920, and is valued at $15,000+. The 16" vanilla colored teddy on the right is from 1910, and valued at $9,000.

The nicest specimen over 30" I have ever seen. Everything about this teddy is artistically correct. *From the Steffes collection.*

As teddy glances to the side he shows his long mohair and brown painted glass eyes. This 32" teddy is a treasure. *From the Steffes Collection.*

On the right front leg of this realistic bear we see the BW tin metal tag from after W.W.I.

"Designed from life," was the theme from 1912 onward for Bing. This 11" long bear on wheels retains that theme into the 1918-1920 years. *The Steffes collection.*

Notice the hump on the grizzly bear's back. It sits higher than his head height. Expressive glass eyes. *From the Steffes collection.* Value is $2,500+.

This pose allows us to view how the wheel rod is attached through two metal discs at the base of his feet. These wheels were made by the Marklin firm for Bing. Dating from 1900, Marklin is a prestigious German toy maker who provided the iron wheels to Bing, Steiff, and most high quality toy producers in the 1900-1915 era. *From the Steffes collection.*

This profile displays the realism of the bear's face and body. *From the Steffes collection.*

A final look at this Bing masterpiece reminds me of their talents. *From the Steffes collection.*

Stands 16" and has desirable cream colored mohair. *From the Steffes collection.* With a silver GBN button under his arm, this 1910 teddy is valued at $9,000+.

One of the more sophisticated looks from this shoe button eyed teddy. Cookies anyone? *From the Steffes collection.*

Who needs props? This creme colored 16″ teddy from Bing is much rarer than the Steiff teddies of the same period. *From the Steffes collection.*

Anyone for tea? The distinctive nose design was done with a cream colored cord to coordinate with the mohair. *From the Steffes collection.*

Sitting in his black forest chair, Bing teddy feels right at home. *From the Steffes collection.* This teddy is near mint, with GBN tag, and is valued at $9,000+.

Celebrating Bing...notice the new member, second from the front. This 20" Bing dates from 1910 and has shoe button eyes. Value is $6,000+.

Another look at the 32" Bing at home. *Steffes Collection.* Value is $15,000.

These teddy bears look well fed. *The Steffes collection.*

The 20″ teddy on the right looks dwarfed next to the 32″ companion. *From the Steffes collection.*

Teddy is taking his teddy for a walk. *The Steffes collection.*

144

Sitting on his favorite log, he patiently awaits. He is prepared to do some "human watching." *From the Steffes collection.*

Which came first, the Bing or the Steiff? The Steiff was made in 1910 and stands 3" tall, with a button in its ear. The 4" Bing dates from 1919, and has the only small white BW tag I have ever seen on his right arm. The Bing also has wire-rod jointing of his limbs, only his head is traditionally jointed. *From the David Douglas collection.* Value of the Steiff is $1,200. Value of the Bing $1,500.

A brassy-cinnamon mohair teddy strikes a special chord among collectors. Rarely seen, this realistic color doesn't surface too often. This teddy is from Lola's Antiques and Bears.Dating from 1920, this 13" teddy is valued at $3,000.

Another view of this special Bing from 1920. *From Lola's Antiques and Bears.*

As the sun sets, we notice teddy's orange-brown painted glass eyes, and his perfect nose. *From Lola's Antiques and Bears.*

One of the four different styles of children's phonographs made by Bing from 1910 through 1925. Called "Pygmyphone," this particular player has special graphics. *Chuck Meek's collection.* Value is $500+.

Notice little Red Riding Hood and the wolf. *Chuck Meek's collection.*

Above the seven dwarfs, we see the phonograph playing a record. Between the two black musicians is the speed control. *Chuck Meek's collection.*

This self contained record player was quite the rage, especially in the roaring '20s. *Chuck Meek's collection.*

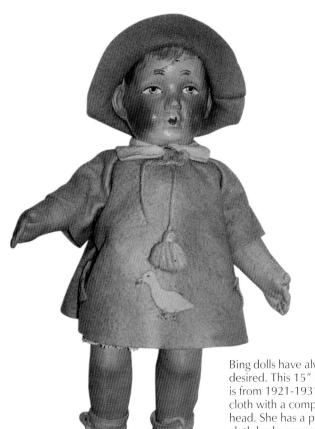

Bing dolls have always been desired. This 15" Bing Art doll is from 1921-1931, and is all cloth with a composition head. She has a pin jointed cloth body, seams down the front of the legs and has Bing on the bottom of her foot. *Catherine Sue McKinney collection.* Value is $750.

A bow tied Bing rests on the fountain. Standing 24" tall, this golden bear dates from the 1920s. *From the Catherine Sue McKinney collection.* His value is $5,000.

A pair of Bings, with contrasting styles. With his bow tie, the 24" teddy dates from the 1920s. The 20" is the sentry style, with feet that appear to be standing on their toes. The rounded head, with ears sewn on the side below the seam, indicate a 1908 to 1912 origin. *Catherine Sue McKinney collection.* Value of the 20" teddy is also $5,000+.

As indicated in the early Bing history, an arrow was affixed to the right ear of the first teddy bears. This 20" teddy has his clamped to the end of his right paw. It is the original mark, perhaps removed and relocated by the seller after the court ruling. *Catherine Sue McKinney collection.*

Sitting on his favorite log, the 20" Bing displays the long pile mohair and glass eyes. *Catherine Sue McKinney collection.*

A closer look at his snout reestablishes the realism which permeated the Bing products. *Catherine Sue McKinney collection.*

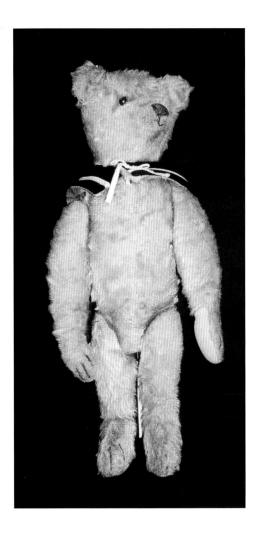

Dating form around 1906, I believe this to be one of the earliest jointed Bing teddy bears. He has tip-toe feet, a long pointed Bing nose, with a perfectly stitched horizontal nose. One of their earliest 12" designs. *Catherine Sue McKinney collection.* Value is $3,000.

This 11" Bing teddy has a very stout body. The orange painted glass eyes and ears sewn up on the head date him to 1920. *Catherine Sue McKinney collection.* Value is $2,000.

A side view shows the great design lines of this 1920 Bing teddy. *Catherine Sue McKinney collection.*

Teddies having fun at home. Contrast the two looks: in front we see the 1906 version while sitting on top is the 11" teddy from 1920. The "Bing Boys" from the Catherine Sue McKinney collection.

This 24" beauty dates from 1920, and has a red BW tag on his wrist. *The Dick and Margie Motzer collection.* Value is $8,000.

A cute 12" teddy from 1914. This is the contrasting style we refer to as "sentry" with pointed toes to stand on. *Dick and Margie Motzer collection.* Value is $3,000.

Still playing after all these years. The
1920s 24" Bing has splendid mohair.
The red glass eyes are replacements.
*From the Dick and Margie Motzer
collection.*

With a red tag on his wrist, he isn't turning his nose up at us, he
was just designed that way. *Dick and Margie Motzer collection.*

A marked contrast in styles. The
conventional 24" Bing, and the
sentry style in a 12". Both bears are
wonderful. *Dick and Margie Motzer
collection.*

The dynamic duo is shown in a moment of repose. Communication is the special dimension designed within each of these Bings. *Dick and Margie Motzer collection.*

A 12" Bing from prior to 1910. Beautiful cinnamon mohair, and shoe button eyes. *From the Lenny Anderson collection. Value $2,500+*

Another look at this early teddy shows ears sewn on the side of the head and perfect paw pads. *From the Lenny Anderson collection.*

The 14" Bing shown here is from the 1920s. His golden mohair has thinned, but be still talks the talk. *Lenny Anderson collection.* Value $2,000.

A slightly different view has teddy reflecting over his nearly 80 years. *Lenny Anderson collection.*

Sweet is the word that teddy brings to mind for me. *Lenny Anderson collection.*

A rare 20" white Bing from 1920. A red BW tag is on his wrist. *Rosemarie Binsteiner collection.* Value $7,500+.

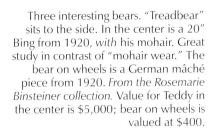

The 20" "threadbear" from 1920 shows us his body design. *From the Rosemarie Binsteiner collection.*

"Threadbear," from 1920. A Bing with a million stories to tell us. *From the Rosemarie Binsteiner collection.* Value is $500.

Another view of the 20" Bing from 1920. *Rosemarie Binsteirner collection.*

Three interesting bears. "Treadbear" sits to the side. In the center is a 20" Bing from 1920, *with* his mohair. Great study in contrast of "mohair wear." The bear on wheels is a German mâché piece from 1920. *From the Rosemarie Binsteiner collection.* Value for Teddy in the center is $5,000; bear on wheels is valued at $400.

Teddy is reading from an 1898 version of *The Three Bears*. This 8″ Bing dates from 1910 and features seamless ears, one of the unique patterns used by Bing. *Pat and Mike Beck's collection.* Value $1,500+.

Bing teddy from 1910. He measures 11"
and has the special ear design, no seams.
Pat and Mike Beck's collection. Value
$2,000+.

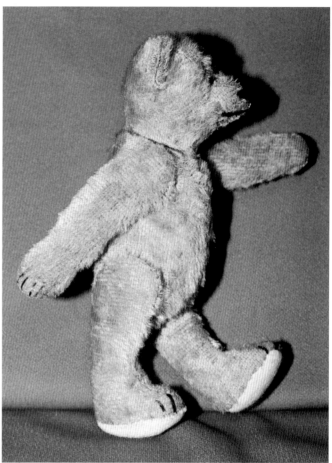

Top left: Wonderful pair of Bings from 1910, measuring 8" and 11".

Top right: The 8" teddy was a favorite Bing early size. This one, like most early versions, has no arm pads, only foot pads. *Pat and Mike Beck's collection.* Value $1,500+.

Bottom left: This front view of the 1910 Bing displays his cute, original smile. Eight inches of special teddy. *Pat and Mike Beck's collection.*

Bottom right: A final look at this 8" Bing gets a parting glance from the tiny shoe button eyes. *Pat and Mike Beck's collection.*

This 12" teddy from 1909 is very special. Even with the overall thinning of the white mohair, this mechanical teddy is very desirable. The silver button on the torso is the GBN (Gebruder Bing Nuremberg) tag. Value is enhanced since the head rotates back and forth via a clockwork mechanism. *From the Mike and Pat Beck collection.* Value is $4,000.

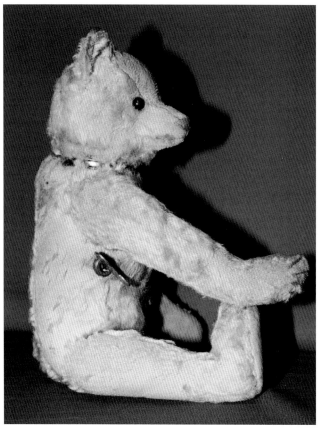

"Sideways Sam," as Pat calls him, shows us his key, located on the other side of his torso from the GBN tag. *Pat and Mike Beck collection.*

Another mechanical teddy bear by Bing. Standing 12", this is the tumbler with hooks at the end of each paw. Dating from 1908-1912, he has a short, cinnamon mohair and a registration button on his torso. *The Pat and Mike Beck collection.* Value is $4,000.

As tumbler teddy stands for us, notice the detailed nose and extra long arms. *From the Pat and Mike Beck collection.*

This teddy can hang in the trees. Look who he found...another animal who can hang in the trees. Bing's 8" monkey is also from the 1910 era. *Pat and Mike Beck collection.* Value of the monkey is $400.

Opposite page:
Down from the trees, sitting on his favorite
rock. *Pat and Mike Beck collection.*

Made of short cinnamon mohair, Bing's
monkey has painted brown glass eyes,
just like the teddy bears. *From the Pat
and Mike Beck collection.*

A side view of this primitive Bing
monkey. *Pat and Mike Beck collection.*

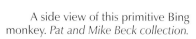

162

This miniature replica comes with its own
beautifully printed box.

Chapter V

Bing's Rebirth

In May of 1992, Eric Kluge was traveling on business in the United States. A local radio station was interviewing him about a unique teddy bear he had repaired, a Schuco Tricky Bear from 1948, which had a pull string voice. Shortly after the program, Eric received a telephone call from an elderly lady who had been listening to the radio. She said she was "living in an old folks home," and asked if he would be interested in seeing some very old teddy bear patterns she owned. These particular patterns originated from her younger days in Nuremberg.

That elderly woman was Frau Sarah Neumann, whose birth name was Bing! Eric was overwhelmed with surprise when he visited Sarah. She pulled out very old teddy bear patterns that had been cut originally from old Nuremberg newspapers. There was an immediate "deal" made and, after a brief discussion, Eric was off with all the patterns tucked safely away in his suitcase. The very first thing that had to be done as he arrived back in Germany, was to register the logo and the company "Bing." It was officially in the summer of 1994 that the rebirth of the old/new Bing Company became a reality. The traditional name of Gebruder Bing Inc. was the name

given for the re-established company.

Frau Sarah Neuman was over ninety years old, but vividly reminisced about her family. She confided to Eric before his departure, that she had come to the United States between the two World Wars. Frau Sarah Neumann has since passed away. The patterns which she held onto for all of those years actually spawned the "rebirth" of Bing. Years later, Eric saw a Bing poster in a Linda Mullins book. Dated 1914, it named Kunz Weidlich as the artist designing the Bing plush animals.

Another lady would play a prominent role in the revival of Bing. Mrs. Herman Weidlich came to Eric and Margot Kluge's doll shop, the Bamberger Puppenklinik. She commissioned them to sell some of her antique dolls, which actually belonged to her daughter, Hilde.

When these dolls were brought to them, Eric was completely unaware of the background of the Weidlichs. It was years later, when Eric met the descendants of the Weidlich family in the United States, that the truth dawned. "As we talked, I started to remember an encounter with an elderly Bamberg customer who's last name was also Weidlich. She

had brought an old doll to be sold," explained Eric. Upon his return to Germany, he learned the lady had died. He located her daughter, Hilde Weidlich-Dittkowski.

Hilde supported the Bing Company, and shared paintings, drawings and countless stories about her father, Herman Weidlich, and her grandfather, Kunz Weidlich. She consented to allow the use of these resources as the Bing company saw fit.

German businessman Eric Kluge has been at the helm of the Bing revival. He was brought up from the very beginning in the toy business. Bamberger Puppenwerkstaette, his parents shop, had to be operated solely by his mother during World War II. His father was drafted into the German Army, leaving his mom as the shop keeper.

The core of the business during the war was the doll clinic. There were no toys available from 1939 until well after the war. Only ten years old when his dad was drafted, Eric helped his mother repair dolls that came to the shop. The time just before Christmas would bring the most work. The most common repair was restringing, with elastic or rubber bands. Supplies were very limited.

ORIGINAL SCHNITT DES ERSTEN **BING**-TEDDYBÄREN (CA. 1907)
ORIGINAL PATTERN OF THE FIRST **BING** TEDDY BEAR (CIR. 1907)

Eric and Margot Kluge beginning the Bing Revival.

One of Bing's new ventures is the Levi Strauss denim teddy. This collaboration celebrates the 170th anniversary of the birth of Levi Strauss.

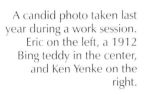

A candid photo taken last year during a work session. Eric on the left, a 1912 Bing teddy in the center, and Ken Yenke on the right.

Another candid photo taken when Ken and Brenda Yenke met with Eric and Margot Kluge in early 1999. We shared information concerning the Bing company. Brenda holds a 1919 Bing; Margot holds a 1912 sentry styled Bing.

Four examples of the blue denim teddies from the Levi Strauss Museum collection. Notice the logo stamped on the teddy's foot.

This giant teddy was recently made by Bing for a museum opening. He is over 15 feet tall...sitting.

Eric and his wife Margot took over the doll business in 1958. This clinic provided a great resource for both antique dolls and teddy bears. This experience is what led Eric and Margot to ultimately get involved with the Bing revival.

Borrowing from some of the past, the myriad of offerings which have been produced by the new "Bing" show the company's genuine effort to revive quality, not quantity! Enjoy the products and experience some of the newly created Bings. A few of the special creations and projects produced so far include:

A spectacular group of teddies created by Bing for the museum opening.

Several teddies from the recent Bing Classic collection.

Konrad, the Cave Bear, commemorating the discovery of the Bing cave by Ignaz Bing in 1905.

"Snappy" is a recent creation from the new Bing company. Each limb is attached by a snap.

Bing recreated this ornament recently. As far back as 1890, Bing made glass ornaments.

Created displays for the Cuddly Brown Museum, Kobe, Japan.

Bing-supplied Huis Ten Bosch theme park in Nagasaki, Japan, the world's largest teddy bear museum.

A new release of a "Gingerbread-bear," originally produced for a gingerbread company in Nuremberg. Bing introduced the famous Kaiser Doll, originally created by Kaemmer & Reinhardt. Bing had bought this firm, but in 1932, with the break up of Bing, they became independent. The original doll was sponsored by Kaiser Wilhelm, the last German Emperor. This recent issue was sponsored by Princess Katharina Von Hohenzollern, a direct descendant.

The Bing Club bear, recently introduced by Bing.

Bing's own design shop, Bamburger Puppenwerkstaette, produced this limited edition bear for the Mercedes Benz company. This little teddy served as a guide on their instructional sales video.

A special edition bear named "Cony" was commissioned by the Bing-Cave association.

Lady Bing is a white mohair teddy with a genuine Gucci purse.

Stephanie is a 16" doll produced just as the first one had been made in 1925 by Bing. This style is similar to Kathy Kruse, a German doll maker.

A Christmas ornament housing a teddy has revived memories of the 1905 Christmas ornament production Bing was famous for.

Some of the old Bing magic is recreated with "Wild Willy," a teddy on a wind-up scooter, and a rotating top.

A Levi Strauss teddy bear is the first ever to be made from denim. Watch for future Levi Strauss/ Bing designs!

I think you will agree—Bing's quality and unique designs are back!

If you wish to contact the present day toy company, Gebr. Bing Inc., the address is:

Gebr. Bing Inc.
Zwerggasse 1-3
96047 Bamberg
Phone: (09 51) 2 29 78
Fax: (09 51) 2 19 41

"The Banker" is another recent Bing creation.

With their own cinnamon cookies, these two Bings are replicas of the 1920 teddy.

Blonde mohair is used on this set of 1920 replicas by Bing.

In the Bing tradition, standing in front
of a page from the 1914 catalogue is
a replica Bing doll from that era.

1996 Bing doll replicas. Cloth body, disc-jointed, and human hair over the poured papier-mâché head.

What a beautiful face on this 1925 replica. Original design was by Kunz Weidlich.

Bing seems to have revived two more
great faces with these dolls.

Photographs by Dave Coleman
Computer Service, Jane Russell